Side by Side

tanka pairs

Larry Kimmel & Joy McCall

Keibooks
Perryville, Maryland, USA, 2018

Side by Side, tanka pairs
Copyright 2018 by Larry Kimmel and Joy McCall

Cover credit, 'Two Coffee Mugs Side by Side," by Thomas Ulrich, Lobo Studio, Hamburg, Germany, courtesy of Pixabay. Used under Creative Commons CC0.

All rights reserved. No part of this book may be reproduced in any form or by any means, except by a reviewer or scholar who may quote brief passages in a review or article.

ISBN-13: 978-1979097635
ISBN-10: 1979097631

Also available for Kindle.

Keibooks
P O Box 516
Perryville, MD 21903
http://AtlasPoetica.org
Keibooks@gmail.com

*no phones rang
to fracture Sunday's calm,
I make my way
in this do-nothing
world*

*and still . . . still,
there is friendship
and there are tanka
and Larry and Joy
will keep me company*

Sanford Goldstein, age 92, Japan

Dedication

*To Sanford Goldstein and M. Kei
—our good friends*

Table of Contents

poets' note 9
glass half full 13
running on empty 14
the silence of origins 15
hunt 16
off-stage 17
old themes 18
living out the days 19
bells 20
midnight koi 21
too late 22
prayers 23
ink and rum 24
leaking into eternity 25
sightless eyes 26
redneck 27
lilting 28
clothes (don't make the man) 29
telling tales 30
keeping the faith 31
fooled 32
last words 33
inside 34
vigil 35
the clock ticks on 36
what now? 37
November sky 38
looking for my place 39
in the cracks 40
entropy 41
shadow 44
gristle and sinew 45
we write 46

two hermits	47
broken	48
brief	49
giving	50
tiny	51
Notes Found in a Hollow Tree	52
the bottom line	66
Amherst	67
high wires	68
diminuendo	69
tracks	70
closed	71
here be dragons	72
clamour and din	73
the light breaking	74
winding down	75
overcome	76
raw nerve	77
a stranger's hands	78
disbelief	79
ink	80
off the edge	81
passing time	82
prowling	83
no wonder	84
music	85
in the middle	86
askance	87
gutter	88
along the avenue	89
falcons	90
belief	91
old ones	92
blundering	93
easing	94
what's the point?	95

medicating	96
too much work	97
rest in peace	98
spinning	99
up the steeple	100
a good cry	101
the bottom line	102
night	103
niche	104
throwing stones	105
coyote and branch	106
dissonance	107
binned	108
home	109
is that all that I am?	110
ripples	111
feral	112
round the bend	113
Afterword, by Lynda Monahan	115
Biographies	117

Poets' Note

Joy and Larry met each other in the pages of tanka journals a few years ago, and became friends and began to write together, almost always in pairs of tanka, and mostly thrown down in passing.

Some fifty years earlier, they both wandered the streets of Amherst, Massachusetts, hung out in the cafés and bars and libraries, sat in the college quadrangle where Robert Frost walked for so many years.

They walked past the house of Emily Dickinson. They sat on the Quaker burial hill just outside of town, finding peace there.

Larry had occasion to go to the local hospital where Joy was working as a nurse and where her daughter was born.

They both visited the Shinto shrine in a nearby town. Joy took her newborn daughter up the shrine steps for a blessing. Forty-five years later, those same steps appeared on the cover of Sanford Goldstein's book *Four decades on my tanka road* (photo by Stanford M.

Forrester, published by Larry at Winfred Press).

Amherst is a small place, mostly inhabited by college students. It is hard to imagine that the two poets did not pass each other on the street, or sit in the same café on the same morning, drinking coffee.

And yet . . . they have no knowledge of meeting there, and would they have known each other so long ago?

There are mysteries we will never grasp. The room we enter a moment after a stranger has left. The trees that cast shadows of leaves and man. Things that don't quite happen, that might have . . . .

Larry Kimmel & *Joy McCall*

glass half full

in pain
I rant and rave
at all the gods
in vain — they are silent,
balancing on pedestals

        I don't have to take this
        lying down, could recline —
           my glass of Guinness
              half full
           soon to be empty

Side by Side

running on empty

on borrowed time
with the ink gauge running
on empty—
sometimes ready for next things
sometimes not

I turn a corner
blind to the dangers
that lie ahead—
in the gutter silt
a wild violet

the silence of origins

above us
a solar-powered plane
almost silent —
one small step closer
to the blue heron

our barnstorming days
over — under
a blue October sky
we return
to the silence of origins

Side by Side

hunt

when coyotes hunt
it's like the worst dog fight
you ever heard—
eerie & wild
to the tenth power

the same howling
echoes in my flesh,
needles and knives
tearing nerve from sinew
sucking marrow from bone

off-stage

the full moon
calls out the common moth
it leaves white dust
on the windows
where the oil lamps burn

how the ghost called
my grandmother's name
one Victorian night
almost my own memory—
so much of life, off-stage

old themes

again the sparrows
that haunt the sidewalk café
again the eroticism
of sunlight through a blouse—
make the old themes new!

at the bar
the red-haired girl fiddles
with her nose ring
she is covered in tattoos
and strangely beautiful

living out the days

grubby fishing boats
moored along the river
far from the sea
tired old fishermen
living out their days

might have known
this would happen—
not a hermit's hut
above the clouds, but a van
down by the river

Side by Side

bells

willow ware
and it all comes back—
skipping stones across
a shaded stream,
distant cowbells

church clock
strikes the noon hour
small feet
paddling in the creek
playing hooky from school

midnight koi

in the still
of the midnight koi pond,
the shadow wing
of a luna moth brushes
the moon

the ghost fish
rises to the bait
swallows
a handful of stars
and the edge of the moon

Side by Side

too late

gathering
long hawthorn spikes
for the spell
drops of blood
on the white page

scrying the brownish stain
my blood runs cold—
what have I done?
too late   too late
the die is cast

prayers

when I cross my fingers
there are all kinds of prayers
and magic built in —
Buddha, Odin, St. Winifred . . .
you name 'em

Boudicca still
rules in my land
warrior queen
yet, to Odin
I sacrifice limbs

Side by Side

ink and rum

warming saké
by the fire, reading
Neruda
I change my mind . . .
hot buttered rum

surrounding
this cocoon of cozy
total night
inkwell
for the poet's pen

leaking into eternity

coffee shops & tanka,
late night thoughts,
the makings of my dailiness—
little by little,
leaking into eternity

left behind
the dregs and stains
a smoke trail
of faint, curling
disappearing words

sightless eyes

a bench
by the village pond
wind and rain
under the dripping willow
a sodden drunk and his dog

as the working class,
with the sightless eyes
of statuary,
search the sidewalks
for a penny of meaning

redneck

the neighborhood
is sun-drunk and the natives
are restless —
just a good ole redneck
holler-day

*tattooed pagans
strutting their stuff
in club-town
cheap vodka and crack
fake pride and joy*

lilting

a cabbage white
shuttles
through tangled brush—
this lilting fabric
at evening's end

it settles
on the lavender
pale wings closing
the cream and mauve
of a silk kimono

clothes (don't make the man)

pink sweater, brown sweater
talking head & nodding head
I call them
Sharon & Karen
you know, sharing & caring

smiling
the good souls I know
wear tattoos
and needle marks
under worn, torn jackets

telling tales

heartsore
his bones shattered
he turns back
to making a living
the only way he knows how

since bone flutes
and bison on cave walls,
whether bedtime tale
or the tv soaps—always,
the storytellers

keeping the faith

waking at night
still that slight aching
in my chest—
some new sadness
digging its way in

fingering the beads
of memory, finding
no fixed interpretation—
only the barred owls
keep the faith

Side by Side

fooled

her surprise at my age
undid
what the mirror
did to me
this morning

the doctor says
it could be worse
and he smiles
I guess he is right
but it could be better, too

last words

tiny moth
above my heart
coiled snake
marking the scar line
where my leg once was

                              a leg lost
                    the tractor repaired—
                             his penciled
                              last words
                            painted over

Side by Side

inside

fever broken,
the child faintly smiles —
fireflies
in
a mason jar

male robins
fighting over a worm
feathers flying
my best friend calls
from the cells again

vigil

dark ravens
cawing in the treetops
waning moonrise
the doe shivers
huddling into dead leaves

all the while
we sit by candlelight
honoring the ritual
of our ancestors—
the vigil by the open casket

Side by Side

the clock ticks on

*the winter wind
wakes me, howling
around the house
I lay awake, pondering
happenstance*

mystics tell us
there are no coincidences—
the hallway clock,
with a certain play in its machinery,
ticks on

what now?

you take a step
and the horizon takes a step
but lately
it seems to be getting closer
—and what if the earth is flat?

it is not death
I fear, but the dying
not the finish line
but that last stretch of road
mined with fear and pain

Side by Side

November sky

they arrive and arrive —
how many starlings
can the old oak
sponge
from the November sky?

one blackbird
singing in the chestnut
before dawn
the nightmares
slip away

looking for my place

take any job, any stance in life
it's part of the puzzle, right?
still looking
for my place
in the big picture

*we are one mote
of the universal dust
inconsequential—
yet how much we matter
to each other*

Side by Side

in the cracks

dry stalks of goldenrod
and Queen-Ann's lace
quivering in winter wind . . .
home
now a derelict house

the light
of an old oil lamp
shining
through the gaps in the wall
of an abandoned barn

entropy
(3 linked pairs)

1.

the night is for the young
and for the solitaries
and I've been both—
soon, I'll step into the midnight forest,
become owl

> *I am branch*
> *bearing that light*
> *featherweight*
> *its great eyes watching . . .*
> *I am the sap, rising*

Side by Side

2.

a terror of biology
shrouded in feathers
I feed on offerings
left at the side of the road
—hawk, I am

I am grass
where the prey hides
trembling
stirring the green blades . . .
I am the sap, rising

3.

entropy gripped me
in its fearful talon
dropped me
in an arid place
I am the hunter, dying

I am the yew
the stalk cut and shaped
the thin arrow
the poisoned bow
I am the sap, rising

Side by Side

shadow

voices close at hand—
hiding the lit cigarette
in the curl of my palm
as a boat slips
through the black of night

heavy footsteps
on the cobbled street
the clink of a chain
I slip into the shadow
of a doorway

gristle and sinew

these aches and pains,
the gristle and sinew
of a disjointed life
coming together
too late . . . too late

body and soul
drawing apart
wondering
of the two,
which is me?

Side by Side

we write

hieroglyphs, cruciform,
ideograms, this alphabet
on and on
on tablets of clay, on papyrus
on parchment, on paper, on screens

alpha
to omega
sparks, beginnings
to our own dark endings
we write, we write

two hermits

*my soul longs
to be a hermit
in a mountain hut
sitting by the fire
living on saké and moonlight*

                                            day's end
                           leaning back I sigh & see
                               behind closed eyes
                             the old porch swing—
                                   hermitage enough

Side by Side

broken

breadcrumbs
stuck in the keys
of the old laptop
how many words can I make
without a s, o, f, g?

doing the math
he loses his train of thought—
broken
he can't even write his name
L rry or hers, J y

brief

in two hours time
the mayfly
takes wing,
mates & dies . . .
a mere haiku of a life

the small brown moth
on my window
every night
called by the lamplight
where I sit writing

Side by Side

giving

back to back,
two pigeons on a balustrade
watching the river—
gift dilemma solved!
bookends

braiding cord
through the holed stone
adding a bell—
the witches' amulet
for my friend's front door

tiny

what if I
could miniaturize
myself—
go native
in a ground berry patch

                    or build myself
                    a hut in heather
                    thin grey smoke
                    from my chimney
            rising up through the purple

Notes Found in a Hollow Tree
(a 14-paired fable)

1. the bridge

on the bridge
dropping Pooh-sticks
into the stream
part child, part woman —
the river between the banks

                    the skipping stone
                hits the farther bank—
                      someday I too
                  will cross the bridge,
            enter the forever wood

2. the stone

in the clutch of oak roots
a sunken tombstone
with my name—
the expiration date
blurred

here in these woods
a broken lichened stone
'now lettest thou
thy servant
depart in peace'

3. the slipper

a damp patch
wild mushrooms and nettles
gather sticks
and light the fire, friend
I'm hungry

                                      a lady's slipper
                                     in utter solitude
                                             I pause,
                                would linger long,
                             but I've a chore to do

4. the charm

damping down the fire
sitting against an oak
my hand settles
on moss and earth
and . . . a dirty old coin

an ancient loss
our good luck charm
on this forest trek
the only coinage
flint for fire, the skill to use it

5. the voice

grey as bark
the strange owl blinks
and disappears—
a tree speaks
and we are spellbound

what voice is this
'who steals my gold?'
a sudden chill
rises from the ground
my blood runs cold

6. the unspeakables

*it is best
to turn away
and not look back
there are pale lights
dancing up ahead*

to advance or to hide—
what would the night creatures do?
the owl, the fox,
the shape-shifters,
the unspeakables

7. wintergreen

crawling through
inky-dark underbrush, the scent
of wintergreen—teaberries!
for herbal tea
we stuff our pockets with leaves

by the night-fire
the heavy pot
rainwater
berries and sugar
fermenting . . . oh, breathe deep!

8. grace

*the fallow doe
comes closer, stepping
from the brush
out of the shadows
sniffing the air*

                        silently following
               her cream-draped fawn—
          at a nothing they dart away
                          such grace
     always just beyond our grasp

Side by Side

9. cool water

dawn—
we have come through
the night,
we drink cool water
from cupped hands

a golden fish
watching us
glides away
slow into the reeds
bubbles rise

10. the light

walking away
again that uneasy sense
we have missed
the thing that matters
the guiding light

                              the path forks—
                    we stand where others
                      have stood before—
             what say you—right into
the heart of the forest dark?

11. broken doll

deep in the forest
a boot print and a broken doll
is there nowhere
someone hasn't been
before us?

the cracked doll
still cries 'mama'
and up ahead
heavy footfalls stop
and turn back

12. running, hiding

shaking off
the cobwebs and moss
and empty fears
I run ahead
calling — come!

                              making myself
                        slender as a sapling
                                    I hide
                        crossing my fingers
that no bogeyman appears

Side by Side

13. snagged

look!
that bit of red yarn
snagged
on the ironweed thorns—
haven't we been here before?

going
round in circles
we gather
the purple flowers
to leave a trail

14. lost

I will mend my skirt
when we get home
the jagged tear
reminds us —
pay attention to the path

                                        when we get home?
                                            at this rate
                                        we'll be lucky
                                                to find
                                    a gingerbread house

the bottom line

the river, all
trickle & bone
the leaves pant
each grape
a raisin

the stream
running high
over its banks
green frogs
crowd the footpath

Amherst

again, lining the street,
crab apple blossoms
the color
of raspberry sherbet—
I never tire of them

cheap whiskey
in the basement bar
at Psi U
Jim Steinman on piano
Robert Frost old and asleep

high wires

high on a hill
two wires sing,
wind or no —
at dusk it's worth the climb
to listen

*why can't I be
a wire strung tight
singing
feeling the slight weight
of swallows?*

diminuendo

the longest day
begins with grey skies
and pain
the year and me
winding down slow

                        once
               so loose and easy,
          my grip tightens
              as the long
     diminuendo narrows

Side by Side

tracks

the gleam
of trolley tracks
under winter streetlights—
a cigarette's
orange glow

night train
still, beside
the empty platform
a man steps
out of the shadows

closed

afterwards
her battered mind
like a bruise
on the thigh
of intimacy

his tears fall
on his own hands
his fingers
his only lovers
behind the cell door

here be dragons

scrying
the marbled linoleum
with unfocused eye—
a cloud-like-morphing
bestiary

April sky
sailors' warning
of hailstorms
the clouds shapeshift—
dragons, breathing fire

clamour and din

I'm in a crowded
Amherst café
lousy with students
—god bless them—
but I can't hear myself think

me, I'm
in a quiet holy room
in Norwich
and still . . . my mind
is filled with clamour and din

Side by Side

the light, breaking

the light
is just breaking
over the hills
here —
a pale grey-lavender

*our skies
are dark,
our trees bare
a light snow is falling
the sun a thin, pale wash*

winding down

just finished my brunch,
but think I need
a little something
to tuck in the edges
a scone sounds about right

my life
winding down slow
that little something
small poem books
a scattering of tanka

Side by Side

overcome

walking
toward Locust Street
the two-story Court House
slowly slowly swallows
St. Michael's steeple

the bronze age burial mound
annoying the Viking warriors
the invaders
built their great castle
on top of the ancient bones

raw nerve

I am a raw nerve
in a cold wind
today
I am a touch-me-not's pod
about to burst

tightly curled into myself
a morning glory
at dusk
showing nothing but the shell
hiding my soul in the dark

Side by Side

a stranger's hands

an unknown someone
has bought my book —
so weird
to be in the hands
of a stranger

*surprised
by letters of praise
for my new poems
I am blind to things
other people see*

disbelief

stunned
by news of his death —
twice finding myself
waiting for the light to change
where there is no light

sitting beside her grave
reading for the hundredth time
the name, the date
'much loved'
my heart still unbelieving

Side by Side

ink

a tat
with an ink like never before
—muted tomato-yellow—
nearly asked her
to show it complete

the small brown butterfly
in the place no one sees
except
for lovers or doctors
or the quick moving spider

off the edge

I prefer
a flat world—
might come a time
to walk off the
        edge

the trouble
with the horizon
is that it runs away
as fast as I walk
towards it

Side by Side

passing time

stoop sitting,
I plan new life-times—
after all these years
still out-running
my headlights

creeping forward
racing backward again
the future a changeling
looking nothing
like the past

prowling

I'm off
to prowl the kitchen
stalk
the wild fridge
raid the pantry

and I
blood sugar rising
at the thought of it all
drink warm saké
and sing

Side by Side

no wonder

that's
what I do
after you go to bed
you know,
I watch movies

no wonder
there's crazy noise
in my dreams
battle cries
and howling wolves

music

here
on the Oriental
where the body lay
moonlight
on dusty piano keys

in the back room
behind the closed door
an old old man
sighing, weeping
playing a cello

Side by Side

in the middle

reading
hometown obits
online—
the surprise
of a middle name

finding out
after he died
that the w. b.
stood for nothing
but w. b.

askance

*she slips
one thin silk strap
from her shoulder
and smiles, leaning
back on the bar*

                        he looks right and left
                        for oncoming trouble
                                      'cause
                            this is too good
                                to be true

Side by Side

gutter

*slow
the evening passes
till closing time
she is standing outside
under the streetlight*

across the street
in the shadow of a maple
a cigarette's orange glow
swells . . . then arcs to fall
in the gutter

along the avenue

a gaggle
of giggling co-eds
brightens the afternoon—
cherry blossoms
along the avenue

surly boys
in school uniforms
scuffing their black shoes
kicking gravel
on the sidewalk

Side by Side

falcons

the intruder
swoops down
on the nest
stealing the food
meant for the fledglings

                                    I'm rolling up
                                        my sleeves
                                          right now
                                  nobody messes
                                    with my chicks

belief

for me, for you
for everyone
kindness
is the better path
to tread

what else
on this journey
of life
matters more
than love?

Side by Side

old ones

it's still dark here
and I haven't stuck my head
out the door yet
it's time to feed the wild cat
and coffee for me

before dawn
I feed the birds
and the mice
and go back to sleep
while the sun comes up

blundering

I am not
too embarrassed
to make
a mistake
in front of you

let us make
blunders and gaffes
and let our faults
and faux pas tumble
and blot all the pages

easing

coffee and chocolate
is a nice way
to spend
a few reflective moments
in the afternoon

honey on toast
and saké by the fire
with poems
is a good way
to ease into evening

what's the point?

I'd like to believe
there is a point to it all
so I do
but I don't know
what it is

I know what
I'd like it to be
I'd want God
to be Love
as the good book says

Side by Side

medicating

I drank down
a fifth of whiskey
in a half an hour
I could have drunk it faster
but was afraid I'd kill myself

your drunken ghost
stumbling down the road
was it you I saw
from my work window
and called out 'pass the bottle?'

too much work

I stood
on the back porch
and thought
this is the summer
I'll never see

come autumn
we will look back
and wonder
where summer went
and what we did with it

Side by Side

rest in peace

sometimes I think
I should just go out
in the woods
and let the elements
do their work

imagine the peace
of lying among leaves
and slowly, slowly
sinking down
into the good earth

spinning

I can put my mind
on one thing at a time
and then
I have to change gears
to get into the next

gears?
my engines are rusted
and cracked
there's just the slow spinning
of the wheels in the air

Side by Side

up the steeple

Frost once said
there is only space for one man
at the top of the steeple
and he always meant
for that one man to be him

*it's the same with falcons
the spire is a flurry
of screeching
and feathers and blood
on the ancient stone*

a good cry

sometimes
it feels good to cry
but only a little
and not about tragedies
but the gentler sadnesses of life

and sometimes
it's just right to howl
and howl
about the deep sorrows
of suffering and loss

the bottom line

for all my fond
theories and beliefs
bottom line
I've not a clue to what goes on
in this universe

for all I know
we slip back and forth
stuck in the middle
of the parallel spaces
neither here nor there

night

I like my hours
alone at night
me and the owls
and a dog
on a distant hill

fox cubs
racing round the trees
city sirens
and the wind
scattering words

Side by Side

niche

wanting
to curl up
in a small ball
like the hedgehog
prickly, snuffly

snoring the afternoon away
in a garden niche if only
the slings and arrows
of outrageous fortune
would let me

throwing stones

at the campus pond
throwing a stone
to the farther bank
for the sheer heck of it
—wavelets rock the mallards

slapping the hand
that threw the stone
I'm always
firmly on the side
of the underduck

coyote and branch

all night long
loud wind and rain
keep me awake
at dawn, a coyote
howls me to sleep

I wake reluctantly—
the *scritch-scritching*
of a walnut branch
at the window bids me return
to dailiness

dissonance

the music
lasted longer
than the marriage
and still it plays
scratchy in my head

heart seizing
he doubles over
mid-wedding march
squashing the organ keys . . .
the dissonance, the dissonance

Side by Side

binned

*sitting through
a poetry reading
I think
there are some who should
and some who shouldn't*

one haiku
after another—
the disposing of tissues
from box
to bin

home

home from hospital—
where there were sticks
apple blossoms
crowd
the window

coming home
to an alien world
after the crash
nothing
is the same

Side by Side

is that all I am?

a name
and a handful of memories
is that who I am
what I am
all I am?

crumbling gravestones
leaning into ivy and grass
no one comes here
a century gone
and those names forgotten

ripples

we are fools
no matter how wise
we seem to be
look at stars and grass
and seabeds

                         don't forget the trees
                      the great trees too huge
                        to hug, who've seen
                       generations passing
                    like ripples on a stream

Side by Side

feral

beware
of feral poets
that lurk in the woods
muttering
'now I must feed'

'I wandered lonely'
tossed scraps
to hide my scent
'do not go gently'
'oh captain, my captain'

round the bend

don't
take this
the wrong way
but where were you
all my life?

I was
round the bend
over the hill
waiting
for you

Afterword

Joy McCall and Larry Kimmel's tanka collection, *Side by Side*, brings together two lives, two places, two poets' voices who give us two ways of seeing. Side by side and yet the poems flow one into the other, creating a beautiful confluence, like the place where two rivers meet. A confluence from which something important emerges—a merging of poetic vision that blends musical clarity and a lush use of language in poems such as 'midnight koi':

in the still
of the midnight koi pond,
the shadow wing
of a luna moth
brushes the moon

> *the ghost fish*
> *rises to the bait*
> *swallows*
> *a handful of stars*
> *and the edge of the moon*

Side by Side

These poems share the grace of growth and experience and a wry awareness of our own brief destiny. Joy McCall and Larry Kimmel, Side by Side in a confluence that celebrates the ceaselessly changing self.

Lynda Monahan
author of *a slow dance in the flames,* w*hat my body knows,* and *verge*

Biographies

Joy McCall grew up in England, moved to Amherst, Massachusetts, and then on to Canada for a couple of decades before coming back to where she was born in Norwich. She thinks that home is where she happens to be at the time, as long as she finds poetry and nature and love there.

Larry Kimmel grew up in the rural area near Johnstown, Pennsylvania. He holds degrees from Oberlin Conservatory and Pittsburgh University, and has worked at everything from steel mills to libraries. He has been publishing poetry for 40 years, and now lives quietly with his wife in the hills of western Massachusetts.

In *Side by Side,* Larry Kimmel & Joy McCall invite the reader into their shared poetic world of crumbling gravestones and bison on cave walls, pagans and feral poets, fireflies and dark ravens. And that's just mentioning a few of the many riveting scenes and encounters found within these pages. *Side by Side* is strewn with gems, offering beautifully crafted responsive tanka pairs by two of the most exciting voices of the form. A privilege, not to mention pleasure, to read!

—Caroline Skanne, editor of *hedgerow: a journal of small poems*

I suggest you read these fine poems slowly, a sip at a time the way you would a fine whiskey. Notice how the voices of the poets blend, become one until the reader pays no attention at all to whether the "author" of a particular tanka is Kimmel or McCall, two poets whose paths must have crossed decades ago when they both lived in Amherst, Massachusetts. Tanka brought them together a few years ago when they were a lot older and a little wiser, both of them tempered by life. This collection is the result. Enjoy.

—Tom Sexton, former Poet Laureate of Alaska; author of *I think Again of Those Ancient Chinese Poets*, and *For the Sake of the Light*, and *A Ladder of Cranes*.

23845547R00069

Printed in Poland
by Amazon Fulfillment
Poland Sp. z o.o., Wrocław